CLIP CLIP CLIP

Three Stories about Hair

by Kathleen Krull

illustrated by Paul Brewer

Holiday House / New York

Kevin's hair was always getting into his eyes, and he liked it that way. He liked it a lot better than the idea of anyone cutting his hair.

"Are you sure this won't hurt?" Kevin asked Azar, the hairdresser. The mirrors were making him nervous. Frightened stares came at him from every direction.

"It's just hair," said Azar. "You'll see," and she started to clip, clip, clip.

Kevin closed his eyes. There were too many pairs of scissors lying around.

"How do I know it will grow back?" Kevin asked her one more time.

It was hard to be brave, with a stranger scraping a cold comb against his scalp. It was a challenge to sit still, with hairs tickling his neck. It was impossible to make normal conversation, with a wet head.

Kevin thought about how the first caveman must have felt when he got the first haircut.

"Whose idea was it to start cutting hair, anyway?" he asked. No one answered. All the blow-dryers were too loud.

He peeked at all the other hair victims. People with wiry hair were trying to make it silky. Those with straight hair wanted it poofy. Those with long hair were getting it cut off, and those with short hair were growing it out.

Many carried pictures
of movie stars and demanded
the same hairdos.
    No wonder hairdressers
were so busy.

Kevin thought about aliens from other planets.
They always seemed to be hairless.
That meant: no haircuts.

"Those people are getting their hair dyed," Azar said. She pointed to a woman with black hair that was turning red. In the next chair was a man with brown hair turning blond.

"Killing their hair?" Kevin gasped.

"Relax—it's just hair," Azar said. "Have a magazine."

The smells of all the different shampoos made Kevin's whole face twitch. He flipped through pages of photos full of . . . hair.

Kevin looked back up at the mirror again. "You scalped me! Don't I look bald?"

Everyone said he didn't. Then he looked down. Old, dead hair! All over the floor! It was a disaster area.

Azar swept it up.

"Could I have some of that?" Kevin asked.
"After all, it's mine." He kept some inside
a plastic bag and took it home.

Kevin keeps it in his drawer, to remind
himself whenever he goes for a haircut:
it's just hair.

Or is it?

"When I woke up yesterday," Ramon said, "my morning hair made my whole family scream."

"Getting gum in my hair," said Lisa. "That makes *me* scream."

"Well, combing out the tangles makes *me* scream," said Ramon. "Then my hair plugging up the shower drain makes my dad scream."

"Finding a hair in my breakfast," said Nina. "That really makes me scream."

Ramon's voice got louder. "And then the haircut my little sister gave my baby brother—clip, clip, clip! That made my mom scream."

"Trying to get hair to behave makes me scream," said Tim. "Hair has a mind of its own."

"Anyway," Ramon said very loudly, "on the bus to school, I got in trouble for laughing at the driver's new hairdo. And at lunch I couldn't eat because I was next to someone whose hair was too greasy."

"I can't eat when I'm next to someone with too much dandruff," Tim said.

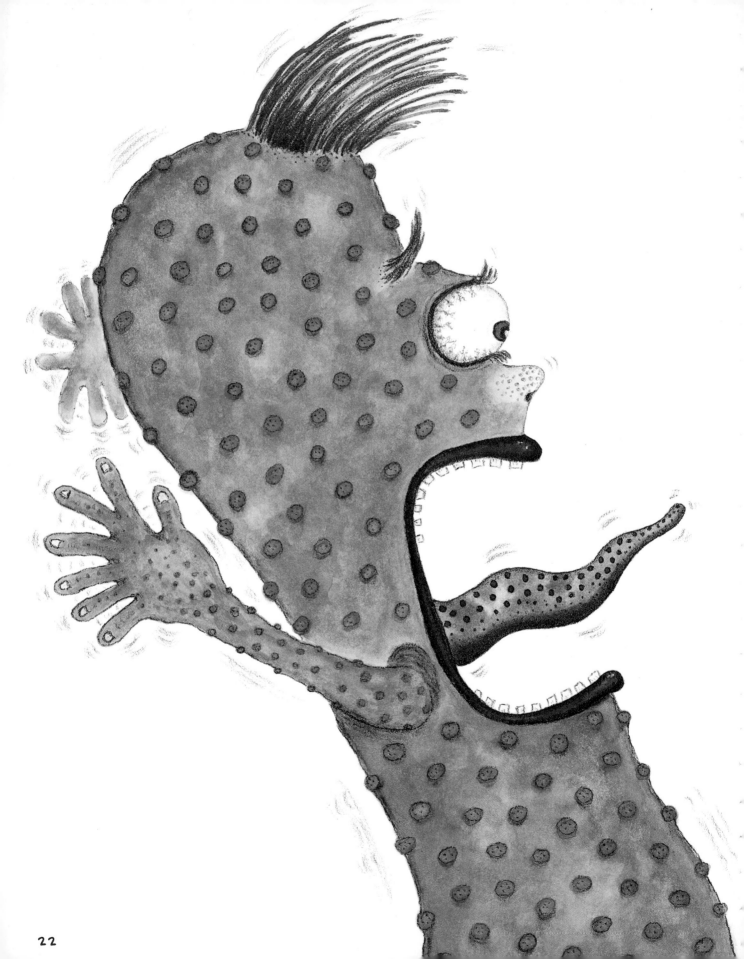

"On top of everything else," Ramon said, getting even louder, "I got stuck behind someone with big hair at the movies. The hairy monster in the movie made me scream. I had nightmares all night."

"Then what?" said Nina, Tim, and Lisa.

"Then this morning, my morning hair was so scary it would have scared the monster from the movies!"

"Aaaahhh!" screamed Ramon's friends.

Helen's Book of Dos

I ♥ LOVE my Hair

I love my hair.
When it behaves, I play
with it when no one
is looking.
    I hate my hair.
When it goes crazy, I'm
frozen under a spotlight
all day long.

I HATE MY HAIR

Other people's hair is just as interesting as mine. Lots of my friends have hair with flair. I'm making a book with pictures of all the hairdos I know.

Oh, I know hair isn't who you are inside. Wild hair doesn't always mean a person is wild. Same thing with wispy hair. But have you noticed some people have bouncy hair and playful smiles to match? Or dreamy hair and dreamy brains to match? Some people seem disturbed by their hair, and it disturbs me, too.

Parent hairdos can be very interesting.

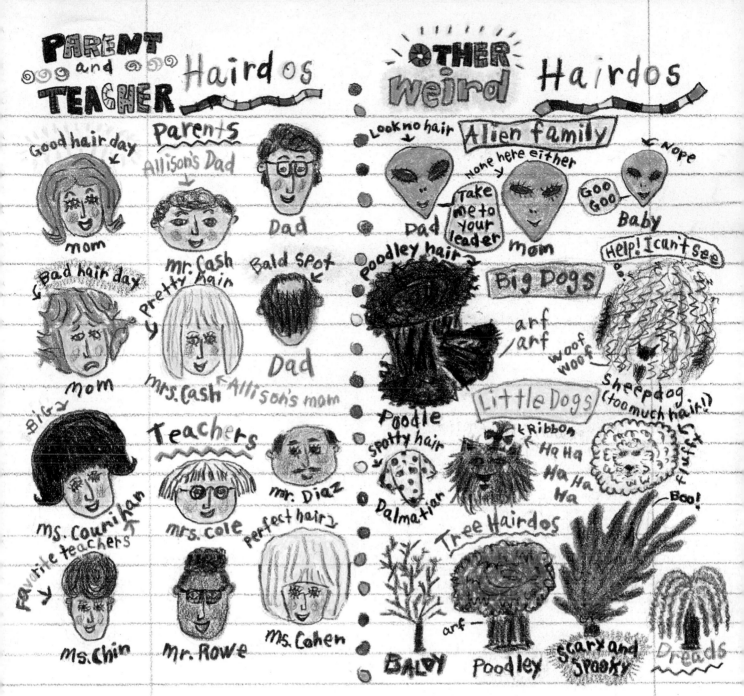

Teacher hairdos can be entertaining. This is the funniest page in my book.

Hair is everywhere. Even trees can have hairdos, if you really look.

What is the cutest thing about babies? Their hair. The best dolls have real hair. The best pets have the best hair. The best stories mention hair a lot, like Rapunzel.

TV and movie hair has to be just right. Rock stars have rebel hair. People who read the news have hair that doesn't move. Movie stars can be famous just for glamorous hair.

To learn everything about hair and hairdos could take up the rest of my life. Already I know these things:

Clip—You just can't predict hair. It's always full of surprises.
Clip—Everyone wants a kind of hair they don't have.

And I know that, clip, secretly
most people think about hair just
as much as I do.

Some Hair Dos and Don'ts

"The average person will spend seven to eight years combing, drying, and fixing their head of hair." —*The New York Times*, December 27, 1997

- Most people will get several hundred haircuts during their lifetime. Your hair grows about six inches a year. Boys' hair grows a little faster than girls'.

- You are not alone if you get a haircut you don't like once in a while. Nothing seems worse. Every minute of every day, you will be red with embarrassment. But we all need haircuts. Otherwise we would all have Rapunzel hair.

- Shampoo is your friend. Bugs like dirty hair.

- Avoid hair emergencies. Although it can be hard to resist cutting your siblings' hair, serious injury could result. Don't even think about trying to cut your own hair. No one will be pleased, especially you.

- Does hair have emotions? Yes, when something gives you the creeps and your scalp tingles. This happens when the muscles attached to the hairs cause the hairs to stand up, almost like they're dancing.

- Does hair give you emotions? Yes, you might cry when your hair gets pulled. Patting someone's hair can be so soothing it can put a person to sleep.

- In general, opinions of hair are best kept private. As funny as parent hairdos can be, it is not a good idea to say so. Never say anything to teachers, especially the bald ones, about their hair.

- Although it is a lot of fun to play with your hair, it can drive people crazy. As much as you might want to play with other people's hair, don't. Instead, grow up to become a hairdresser.

- Hair is really important to many people. In the U.S.A., people spend 22.4 billion dollars a year on their hair.

- If you make your own book about hair and hairdos, it is guaranteed to be different from anyone else's.